Getting Un-stuck!
"Dancing Through Your Storm"

Life isn't about waiting for the storm to pass it's about learning to dance in the rain...... "Vivian Green"

Dedication:

This book is dedicated to my little princess Evenise, and to my best friend Mia.

Evenise,

I will always push and guide you with love and support to assist you with living up to your full potential. Never settle for anything less than you deserve. Always remember to treat people exactly the way you love being treated. Regardless of their differences in race, religion, gender, sexual orientation, age, or any other factor; treat them all the same and with love. Remember, our differences give us our own personal sparkle.

Mia,

Thank you for keeping your spirit close to me when I need it most. I'll never forget that horrible day in July of 2007 when your life was taken. I'll also never forget the ten thousand good times we had together. You always know when to come my way and fill me with your warm and loving spirit. I know that you hated the thought of traveling by plane, but I've taken you with me on every trip I've taken since your transition into the spiritual realm, and you know I travel a lot. Continue to be my guardian angel. Buckle up and enjoy the ride. We have much more to experience.

Love you both! ☺

Lalita

Table of Contents

Chapter 1: How did I get here? 6

Chapter 2: The Beginning "Where do I even start?".............24

Chapter 3: Know Who You Are: Having a Solid Foundation .37

    Including Ten Steps to That Solid Foundation...........37

Chapter 4: Acceptance and Being Present............................50

Chapter 5: Balancing the Yin and Yang 57

Chapter 6: Now what? Taking That Next Big Step 63

Chapter 7: Pay Attention 68

Just a few people I'd like to thank!.......................................76

References and Suggestions...78

CHAPTER I

How did I get here?

My goal for you:

I want this book, "Getting Un-Stuck," to be a life-changer for you. Specifically, I hope to help you make your way through any challenges you face with a smile – while you chart the road through and out of your challenges.

In this book, you will learn how to develop valuable skills that will help you tap into the great powers within you, at the moment you need them most. Some of the methods I took that assisted me with working my way through a few of my own storms will be shared over the next few chapters. Yes; you read that correctly, "a few of my own storms." One thing I've learned over time is that life will continuously throw you curve balls when you least expect it. However, with the right tools and methods, you will quickly be reminded that no storm lasts forever. You will also learn that you already subconsciously possess the skills to conquer any challenge that come your way. Once you complete these chapters, you will be able to face any challenges or storm in a different and more productive way!

How I came to write this book:

Why did I write this book? Let me explain. I currently live and work in Arizona. The book came about because of the difficult process I went through in dealing with a situation I encountered before I relocated. This situation, and my experiences dealing with it, motivated me to take a chance, and move completely away from my comfort zone. Before I moved to Arizona, I'm almost positive I applied to 100 different jobs in Chicago, Atlanta, Texas, Guam, and Puerto Rico. Naturally, I grew frustrated with my seemingly hopeless search and decided to say a prayer and affirmation...Send me wherever I need to be, and I promise to make the best out of wherever I am sent. I AM a successful, powerful, and creative, spiritual being. Within forty-five days of me speaking this affirmation, my Ford Explorer was filled to the top with boxes and I was on my way to a completely new life in Tucson, AZ.

Let me be blunt. I moved to Arizona after being blackballed with a group of seven other individuals from a certain sector of the social service arena. Let me tell you about the mess I found myself in. I had worked tirelessly as a contractor for two agencies. I was a home-based case manager for families involved with the Department of Child Services (DCS). My job description was impossible and I was never "officially off of work". Unless, I was out of the country, I had to be available by phone twenty-four hours a day. I can even recall being on vacation in Jamaica, but waking up earlier than my friends to complete monthly reports. I worked with my clients hands-on and in their own homes. My tasks included providing positive parenting classes, supervising visitation, seeking and obtaining housing, assisting parents with finding employment, seeking community resources and providing nonstop transportation services. I also drove some of the parents I worked with to substance abuse treatment centers over two hours from where we lived (I usually worked in my community). My primary duty in this work was either to reunify a family or to minimize the possibility of their children being removed from the home.

After over seven years of hard work, I was a part of a group of people in the agency investigated and accused of false double billing. All of us with the exception of one person to my knowledge were innocent. We were all blackballed due to the actual false billing of one individual. Naturally, I was both extremely upset and embarrassed. I was also confused because I knew the allegations against me were false. My work had been consistently excellent and very thorough. It was so good that I was requested to work 80 to 90 percent of my cases by Department of Child Services workers and their supervisors.

Typically, if a state worker needed a specific service completed or court ordered for a family, they would send a referral to a contracted agency. That agency would in turn choose a case manager or therapist to provide that service. Most of the referrals I received already had my name on them before being faxed or emailed to my agencies. I was known, in short, for my ability to get the job done right. Of course, I had many moments of frustration in this difficult field. But to compensate, I had developed some personal tools that worked for me. These tools included an ability to focus on my work while processing my own personal feelings regarding certain topics. I also found the ability to shift into a higher level of consciousness when I needed to. I had begun to look deeper inside of myself. As often as I could, I would put myself mentally into my client's shoes. Being able to be empathic assisted me with successfully working with them at the level they needed it most. True enough, on some days it drained the life out of me, but my ultimate goal was to provide an excellent service to others in need.

Ever since I was in high school, I knew I eventually wanted to start a business, write a book, and work hands-on servicing people in need. I had fears and self-doubts along with the reaffirmed fear and doubts of friends and relatives. Those concerns convinced me to stick with work that was "stable and secure". I literally learned in less than 24 hours that stability and security outside of self and some higher power were a facade and simply did not exist for me.

Before the group of us were investigated, it was rumored that a few people in the sector were billing for services they didn't complete -- involving several different agencies. At the time, I didn't have an ounce of worry, because I knew I worked very hard and very was ethical. I did whatever was needed, whatever it took to reunify families. Me being very flexible, and having the ability to work with individuals from all walks of life, was one of the primary reasons I was requested on so many cases. I was also seen on a weekly basis in court, family team meetings, professional staffing, etc. So, who would question my work right? Yeah, just keep reading.

At the end of the "audit" anyone who worked for these specific agencies was terminated -- the one known guilty person and several of us who were innocent. Had I listened to the first few signs -- call them pebbles the Universe threw my way as a hint to leave that sector, I would have already been gone during the time of that bogus audit. To clarify what I mean by "bogus" audit, none of the DCS workers, supervisors, or former clients were ever asked directly whether or not I actually provided the service.

Several experiences and conversations later, I realized that finally I had arrived at the time in my life, where I should write some step-by-step tips that would help people get through some of their toughest times with a positive attitude. I knew that I was not alone. I also knew that others could benefit from learning tools that had helped me so much. And so, I present these tools that can assist anyone to transition from chaos to celebration.

The great American comedian, writer and philosopher Dick Gregory said it: *"Fear and God can't occupy the same space."*

The Jump Off:

The foregoing mess made me ask: How did I end up in this situation? I had worked hard for over seven years building relationships and working with families through a very fast passed, high stress level arena of social services. And what seemed like out of nowhere I was out of work and furious. Fortunately, I had already begun practicing mindfulness and meditation. Had I not, I probably would have been near a meltdown or entered a deep depression.

I was heavily influenced at the time by Russell Simmons, Oprah Winfrey, Dick Gregory, and Maya Angelou. All I could think to say was thank you for all the good in my life that kept me going. I remember very clearly that I thanked God at that time for my ability to focus on the positive, remain in a constant state of gratitude, and to be loving. I also developed the ability to embrace my amazing support system. I have been blessed with some very supportive family members and close friends, and I don't take them for granted.

As a result of the audit, I literally had to sit in a jail briefly. Almost two years after I was fired for no justifiable reason, my lawyer called me early one morning to tell me that I was to be served a warrant for theft. My lawyer said I needed to decide whether I wanted to turn myself in or take a chance on being picked up by the police. He told me that the choice was mine.

This was ridiculous to me. I had never even stolen a candy bar, let alone taken money or property under false pretenses. Keep in mind that during this period of my life, I was fully aware of the racism prevalent in America within the legal system. I was aware that too many Black men and women were injured, or even killed when being arrested, including when the arrests were for "crimes" that hadn't even been committed. These murders and beatings were being shown almost on a weekly basis both on television, and on social media. So naturally I questioned whether or not it was my turn?

I made arrangements to turn myself in and to immediately post bail. So, I had to sit in a jail cell for five hours (which felt like an eternity) for a crime that I did not commit. Upon my release, I asked the obvious question:

Now what do I do? First, I wrote out a list of things I was grateful for. Then I thought hard about what my next few steps should be. I knew that as bad as this situation appeared to be, my trouble was only temporary.

I also knew that it would be up to me to take the proper first few steps -- and to be prepared when life would finally be better. I held the firm conviction that despite everything, better days were on the way. This was the faith and conviction that sustained me. It began to dawn on me that these particular circumstances were matters that were meant for me to share with other people. Not to boost my ego or to pose as some great strong person -- but simply to show how with the powers of gratitude, stillness, faith and strength, anybody in a tough situation could endure that situation with a smile and positive attitude.

Eventually, even my "church lady" mother and I were able to crack jokes about my predicament. The conviction grew in me that not only was I a child of an infinite source and spirit, but that the spirit lived within me. Despite my problems, my mind would not process even the slightest thought of failure. I maintained a positive attitude. I still needed to formulate some specific steps in order to prevail and conquer my current situation. Next thing I knew, I was paying my attorney and eager to keep moving forward. I decided that it was time for me to stop procrastinating and take specific steps toward living up to my potential -- to face up to my destiny. I was ready to become a Certified Life Coach. I even considered becoming an author of a self-help book. I had been coaching people in various areas as early as my high school years.

Being an informal coach and teacher also seemed to have followed me on every job that I had ever had, at Arby's Roast Beef, at UPS, and on to every employer that I'd had in social services. But I still questioned whether or not I could become a Certified Life Coach and an author? I had several excuses as to why I probably could not. After all, I didn't have much money. I worked long hours. I didn't really know how to BE a life coach or author. And, honestly, I was just scared. But, thanks to my Creator and the newly developed thoughts, tools, habits, and steps I had developed, things began to fall into place.

I mentioned to my Sunday school teacher, the idea of becoming a Life Coach. That was my subtle way of putting it out into the universe. She introduced me to my first Life Coaching mentor. After meeting with my coach, I decided to purchase a course and become a Certified Life Coach. Purchasing that course was my first big step in investing in myself. I had to take a class and recruit a practice client. Both myself and my client had to complete an array of assignments while showing consistent progress. In order for me to pass the course with full completion, my client had to submit reviews and surveys to the actual instructor, without me being able to review her response—talk about being an anxious wreck. To my surprise, I passed with flying colors. I was proud of myself because I've always hated taking test.

A few weeks after becoming a Certified Professional Life Coach, I mentioned to my Sunday school teacher that I wanted to write a book and asked if she could give me any pointers. Did I mention that she was in her eighties? She teaches me regularly in subtle ways that you have the power to push beyond any perceived mental or physical limitation that you may endure. She invited me to her house for a meeting. We bounced around a few ideas during our meeting, and she gave me some interesting information. She told me about a book writing class that was taking place at the church. Oddly enough, the class was scheduled to take place the one day I had off work that week. How's that for the Law of Attraction?

Take a few minutes to think back. Have you ever put deep thought into something like completing a goal or task, then talked out loud about it, believing it was possible? And then found that things just began to fall into place? Was this just a coincidence or an instance of *Divine Order*? Think of an accomplishment or task you want to complete, big or small, and then give the method I mentioned a try. Think about it, visualize it, speak it out loud -- and be prepared when positive results come your way. The most important aspect is to really believe that your goal is attainable, and to be willing to physically move

YOUR feet. Be ready and willing to shift your mind and heart too.

Despite being nervous I attended the writing class. Surprisingly enough, my words begin to bloom like wild flowers and just flow onto the paper. The instructor put us into an open and honest meditative state. He said that if we allowed ourselves to become *still* and *present* the words would just flow. I didn't believe him …until I started to actually experience it for myself. He stated that people like to read things that make them feel good. He also said that most people have a book stuck inside of them that needed to get out.

Growing up as a 1980's baby in the inner city of Gary, Indiana, I saw all kinds of wild things. For those who aren't familiar with my home town, Gary has been noted to be the Murder Capital of the United States on several different occasions. During the 80's and early 90's, crack cocaine and poverty hit our neighborhoods badly. My old high school, was referred to as Murder High for a few different reasons.

My parents tried to be protective and hide as much as they could from the three of us. But living in a neighborhood filled with crime, drugs and poverty, there was only so much that could be hidden, especially if you have a kid as curious as I was. Even though I had these experiences I LOVE Gary, Indiana. I had an excellent childhood filled with some wonderful experiences. Chicago was only minutes away so I had ready access to the city's museums, two different zoos, various ethnic neighborhoods, and many cultural institutions.

But, growing up in my city, we had to grow numb to or consider it "normal" to live through extremely dangerous and serious situations. For instance, it was "normal" at that time to know that if a car started to slow down, you should prepare to run, because a drive-by shooting might be about to take place. It was "normal" to watch out for broken glass from crack pipes or alcohol bottles when riding bikes -- you had to watch out so you wouldn't puncture your bike tires. It was "normal" to know who the neighborhood drug addicts and dealers were. It was "normal" for the heating system to malfunction at school during winter months. I lived on the corner house of a cul-de-sac on 43rd and Ohio St. I even remember my friend having pizza delivered to my house because the delivery guys had gotten robbed so much in the circle, they refused to deliver down there.

However, despite all these problems and many others, I wouldn't change any of it, Gary bred into me a certain set of strengths, and coping skills. These were strengths and coping skills I probably wouldn't have gained living in a protected, quiet, mostly crime-free suburb. True enough it came with its own set of trauma and paranoia, but I can honestly say that each experience has benefited my life in one form or another, and I am grateful. Realistically, Gary is no different than any other poor inner city. Most people growing up in this type of environment experience similar highs and lows. A solid foundation is imperative for anyone, especially for a person being raised in consistent chaos. My overall foundation assisted me with the skills to process just about anything clearly. Both positive and negative experiences.

Another thing I learned about growing up was hypocrisy and conflicted religious beliefs. For example, the hypocrisy of religious leaders saying one thing and doing another. I can remember various pastors and other elders in the church preaching one message but living by quite different rules. Some preachers spoke against adultery, fornication, homosexuality, addiction or over indulgence every Sunday. But they sometimes had mistresses inside and outside of the church, or frequently abused this or that substance themselves. I also remember hearing in church how "sinful" it was to gossip, but most of the "juicy" gossip I heard came from church members? Even today, a handful of gay and bisexual people that I know date individuals who consider themselves straight, mostly out of fear of being judged.

I was a preacher's kid and raised in church, so I was at one service or another on a weekly basis. I saw the positive and negative experiences that came along with it up close and personal. I'm extremely grateful for my initial spiritual and religious foundation, but I learned over time that all humans are simply a work in progress living by trial and error every day, regardless of what title they may possess. One thing I was sure of, was that people in need gravitated more to individuals that were open and not as visibly judgmental or hypocritical.

I knew as early as elementary school that my purpose in life was to make people feel better, find easier ways to cope, and move through hard times with as much ease as possible. I can remember getting fussed at by my mother because I gave out "the good ice cream sandwiches" to some of my neighborhood friends. I just knew that my friends were hot and sad. And ice cream sandwiches were the perfect treat that always made them (and me) feel better. Instead of telling me not to hand out the ice cream sandwiches anymore, my mother bought less expensive popsicles and told me, "Here pass these out."

I knew that passing out my little freeze pops would make my friends feel better. I liked then and now to help people and make them feel better. From my elementary school days into my adulthood, I really thought that I wanted a career that focused solely on business, however, I always felt more fulfilled when providing service and a helping hand. I would often think to myself, "I wonder if there is a way that I could make a lot of money and still help people."

Back to that writing class, my Sunday School teacher had suggested. Sitting in the class at the time, trying to find balance, going through that particular battle, I found the conviction growing that now was the time to take action and move forward. I had procrastinated long enough. And it was time for me to take another big step towards my destiny. The chapters that follow will explain just how I got "unstuck, and how I decided to help others get "unstuck."

CHAPTER 2

The Beginning
"Where do I even start?"

I would like to focus on three primary factors that will assist you in getting started. Making a solid decision to change your current situation or circumstances, stepping out of your comfort zone, and taking a deeper look into your current circle of influence. These are key factors for dancing out of your storm and becoming unstuck. Until you make a definite unwavering decision to change, you'll continue to walk in circles verses taking steps forward. If you don't consider stepping out of your comfort zone in one form or another, there is a chance that you may continue to do what you've always known. As far as your circle of influence, your actions should line up with the goals you're trying to accomplish.

For example, if my goal is to lose 20 pounds, I should probably interact more with people who are concerned with healthy eating and exercise instead of hanging with people who enjoy going to buffets several times a week without changing their food choices and exercise habits. When I decided to write this book, within two weeks most of my conversations took place with people who write books, edit books, or former English teachers. I now limit my contact with anyone who is consistently negative or who's overall life goals don't line up with mine.

First things first. You have to make a solid decision to change your current circumstances. Almost all of us sooner or later find ourselves in situations that can knock us off our square. That can knock us down and out. That is, unless we have the will and the courage to say: "I'm standing firm. I'm going to ride this crisis out and survive, no matter how bad things get. No matter what obstacles stand in my way."

You may not think so now. But once you learn some good workable techniques, and have made up your mind that you can take charge in life's many storms, nothing will stop you. Sure, obstacles may slow you down. But they won't stop you. It's my belief that all life's obstacles, are only the Universe's way of helping a person shift gears so that he or she can move in different and more beneficial direction. Yes, we all can overcome obstacles and weather the hard times. But how can we do that?

In this chapter, I want to share with you some techniques. Techniques that may be pertinent to your life as they have been to mine. And it's my strong belief that we must not be afraid to hold ourselves accountable. It's also my belief that our individual actions are the only actions that we can control. None of us can control the world outside of, or around us. Fortunately, we all can control ourselves -- but it sure isn't always easy.

One desire of my writing this book is that I want to serve as your life coach. I believe I can help you learn to make better decisions and follow through on those decisions. I also believe that you have the will power to follow through with a set of tools along with a solid support system. You do however have to be willing to take some physical action. No one else can do that for you. Just you. I had to learn that lesson the hard way. The good news is that, although we "alone" must take those first steps, we are never to assume that we are alone in facing life's tests. There is always a higher presence at our disposal. Nor should we ever assume that we are the first person to ever face a particular test, or challenge in life.

What do I mean by fully holding ourselves accountable for our choices? A good example would be in the past when I chose to loan some friends and family members money over the years. I even went as far as allowing certain utilities and other bills to be in my name trying to "help", only to end up having to make a $1,200.00 payment arrangement that I was responsible for paying off, along with taking other hits to my credit. We all know that loaning and borrowing money can cause problems. Especially when doing so against our better judgement. By loaning and borrowing we can get ourselves in situations that cause us to grow angry, lose relationships, and cast blame. When that happens, who's more at fault? The people who constantly ask for money? Or those who continue to lend money knowing that they may not get the money back. And if they do get the money back, the repayment would be much later than promised.

Everyone who knows me personally knows that I am EXTREMELY credit conscience. So of course, I was on fire when I began to receive past due bill notices. In my mind, I had sincerely been trying to help, and I had been let down by the same people I attempted to help. Once I was able to meditate about the situation, do a little writing about the whole thing in my journal, and get my emotions in check about the situation, I realized that I was the problem. I had seen enough examples in the past with their actions where I should've known that things couldn't have gone any other way financially. So why should I have gotten upset with anybody but myself? Once you allow a person to fail to live up to an agreement that you've made, regardless of your relationship to them, it's up to you to cut ties and release yourself from the stress or headache.

People do exactly what they are allowed to do. As I stated previously, the only behaviors you can change are your own. You do not have the power or control to change anyone's actions outside of your own. With that being said, if you continue to make the same mistakes, or choices repeatedly, you choose to allow the possibility of continued stress and headache. We typically experience the same problems over and over again until we learn whatever lesson that is intended for us to learn.

Leaving your comfort zone

Second, a general life rule here is be prepared to possibly leave what has been comfortable for you and establish new norms. Besides, most so-called comfort zones are only an illusion. Remember, I worked in the same employment sector for over seven years before I was pushed out for reasons that were no fault of my own. That was when I realized that most so-called comfort is not only taught, but is a total illusion. That experience with unpaid bills and that treacherous audit are just a few of the many instances that formed part of my learning process and pushed me on to new and better ways of dealing with life. And of finding life brought lessons that I could pass on to other people. I developed an entirely different life in less than two years thanks to that push. I moved clear across the United States knowing only one person, my mother.

Right here I should jump back in time and tell you about an earlier learning experience when I moved out of my so-called comfort zone and entered the world of the unknown. I was 18 years old and still in Gary, Indiana. I graduated high school in June and shipped out for Army basic training in July. As nervous as I was at the time, joining the Army was the only way I knew that would allow me to go to college and move out of the ghetto. I didn't have any other options - at least options that I was aware of. I hadn't taken academics seriously enough in high school to get a college scholarship, and neither of my parents (who were divorced by then) could afford to send me to college. I figured the Army chance was worth taking. The Army National Guard was paying between

70%-100% college tuition as long as I went to school in the state of Indiana.

Two weeks before I left home for Army basic training, I heard a thousand reasons why I should go into the military and two thousand reasons why I should not. All these pro and con reasons came from different people I knew at the time. Some reasons came from adults and some came from peers my own age. The reason I should stay home that will always stick with me most was from Joe Lee. Joe Lee had been one of my close friends since we were in the fifth grade. He was a genius academically but stayed in the streets like most of us. Since living "the street life" was the norm for several of my friends and family members, I didn't have an issue or think that there was anything wrong with his lifestyle at that time. It mirrored everyone else's. All I knew is that he was one of the greatest guys I'd ever met. He always had my back if I needed anything.

I lost track of Joe Lee's reasons why I shouldn't join the Army. I actually agreed with most of them, but felt as though I had no other choice. Within a month or so of my departure for basic training, my mother was mailing me his obituary to Fort Leonard Wood, Missouri's military base. I can't describe the level of pain and hurt I felt reading that obituary. Joe Lee died more than 16 years ago -- and I still feel the same level of pain if I think about him too long. Had I not left home there is no question as to whether or not I would have possibly been with him the night he got shot. My friends and I usually traveled and hung out in packs, so we were either all safe or all at risk of being harmed. Some days I wonder if I'm still alive today because more often than not I listen to my gut. That was one of my most devastating experiences of how sometimes you just have to follow your gut and take that step in a completely different direction.

You might have to move to a new town, sign up for certain groups, seminars, programs, classes, participate in webinars, and anything else outside of your old norm. Growth may not always be comfortable, but it'll always be necessary upon accomplishing your goals. The change may not be too trendy or popular with your current circle so be prepared for possible backlash. Your overall goal should be geared toward self-improvement, not people pleasing. Which brings me to my third point, your circle of influence.

Circle of Influence

Lastly, Circle of Influence. What does your current Circle of Influence look like? Do you all support each other when making positive choices? How is your current circle working for you? Over time you become more like the people you spend the most of your time associating with. Sometimes you may subconsciously pick up each other's personal traits and habits. Think back between the ages of twelve and thirty- five years old. Take personal inventory. What habits and traits did you pick up from your crew? That crew may have been classmates, co-workers, social companions, spouses and family members. Take a few moments to list those things that you absorbed from those you associated with. Be honest with yourself. Take a few moments to list those below. Both good and bad habits (smoking, drinking, partying all night, career choices, church home, spiritual practice, etc.).

Positive:_____ _____ _____

_____ _____ _____

_____ _____ _____

Negative:_____ _____ _____

_____ _____ _____

_____ _____ _____

Even in high school my core set of friends were all similar in one way or another. We all had jobs, had the same sense of humor, kind of rough around the edges, but very goal-driven. We were also known for throwing some of the best parties in Glen Park for our age. I'll save those stories for another time ☺. Till this day, most of us are very close. Experience, circumstances, and maturity have caused a few of us to grow apart, but the love is still there. Being mindful of the people you keep close to you will be important at every age. Keep people around that will guard your spirit as much they do their own. Always return the favor.

What is next regarding your Circle of Influence? Using myself as an example, nine times out of ten most new things I've experienced and have been exposed to have always come from people that didn't even look like me. People that weren't raised like me, not in my same age group, and probably didn't even speak the way I do. The one thing that I consistently did while being true to who I was at the core was to always be open minded.

Even when my safety was questioned in certain instances, I remained open. I lived in areas a good portion of my life where anything could happen, and often wild things did happen. But I knew that regardless of what my environment was there were beautiful people all around. Beautiful people in need of some soul searching. Beautiful people in need of an occasional escape or adventure outside of their day to day to lives. As dark as my neighborhood appeared to be at times, the beach was close, Chicago was close, and a myriad of small local business owners who motivated me to want my own business at some point.

I've traveled to different countries and found more enjoyment hanging out with the locals than I did relaxing at the security protected resort. I have always felt protected by something greater than myself. I urge you to be open to a circle of Influence that pushes you outside of the box, especially when it's for your own greater good. Being surrounded by people who were older and more experienced than myself encouraged me to take some big and important steps outside of my comfort zone.

As we come to the end of this chapter, I want to emphasis; don't be afraid to hold yourself accountable. Your actions are the only actions you can control. Once you make a decision, it's up to you and only you to follow through. Never assume that you are alone. Never assume that you are the first person to ever experience this test. Never assume that you will be the last. Fully hold yourself accountable for your choices.

CHAPTER 3

Know Who You Are: Having a Solid Foundation

Including Ten Steps to That Solid Foundation

If you possess a solid foundation of self and know who you are, you won't have to spend time seeking validation and approval from outside sources. You may be wondering how you can form a solid foundation of self? How can you figure out exactly who you are? Those questions and answers are what you'll find in this chapter. The last half of this chapter offers my ten-step program for developing a solid foundation of self. I believe you'll find this useful.

Some people were fortunate enough to learn lessons of self-worth and foundation in their homes at an early age. While other people experienced pain, and suffering for years while trying to learn who they are and what their worth is. Seeking outside validation can become harmful depending on where you look. Unfortunately, unhealthy sources are usually the easiest sources to find. We may seek validation through use of addictive substances. We may engage in unhealthy sexual behavior. We may participate in some illegal activity for the sake of fitting into a particular group. And you probably already know that these behaviors can be damaging if you aren't careful. Or even if you are careful. Fortunately, as a safeguard against such unhealthy validations, there is power in knowing who you are, who you want to be, and who you don't want to be.

Here's how I learned who I was and am. My parents split up when I was about fourteen or fifteen years old. My dad and I were very close before they separated. But maintaining a consistent relationship with him was a bit of a strain for both of us for several years after. However, my father helped and encouraged me to form an extremely solid foundation within. With his help, I knew exactly who I was. I also knew how much potential I had. Even before I finished elementary school, I knew that I had the ability to be anything I wanted to be thanks to him.

Forming a solid, personal foundation was not without challenges. I recall having to stand in the corner for telling my classmates that Santa Claus wasn't real. As you can see, I've always had a big mouth, well I've always "said it like it is". I said as clear as day. "My daddy said that he and my mama work hard every day, year-round in order to be Santa Claus every day. No man like Santa Claus would come to our neighborhood any day of the year. So why should Santa get credit for coming on Christmas? Besides, we don't even have a chimney." I'm sure I could have found a different way to say it. But I have never understood why a child should be punished at home or at school for telling the truth, or for asking questions in an attempt to learn the truth. One of the best things about growing up with my father was that I knew that as long as I asked him respectfully, I could ask him ANYTHING I wanted to without getting into trouble.

Ultimately, or so I believe, we are all children of an infinite source. Our source has no end and does not see any limitation. I'm not speaking from a strictly religious standpoint here, but from a wider perspective of spirituality. Being a child of God in my opinion provides each of us with a firm foundation, a safe place to turn when rough times come our way. Although I was raised in the church, it wasn't until I was in my late twenties and early thirties that I began to take what I learned from my original foundation and add to it the tools I learned later with Mindfulness and Meditation. My original foundation along with Mindfulness and Meditation combined is what taught me how to fully tune into my own personal Higher Self.

Once you are fully aware of who you are, you are quickly reminded that all things are temporary. Regardless of what the current circumstances may be, emotional pain gets better. That's true especially if you decide to take a step forward outside of your storm. Know that all dots connect. Understanding that concept should eventually put you in a position to be able to look at your problems from the inside out.

For me, it took a while. But I eventually learned to stop and ask myself in the midst of any storm, "What is this lesson here to teach me?" "What do I need to learn out of this madness?" "And what exactly is my role in creating it?"

I was like everyone else before I learned the benefits of embracing the madness. I carefully avoided any headaches or challenges in life. Or, I found a way to move around those headaches and challenges without actually having to fully deal with them. You can imagine the result. Of course, those same challenges, or something similar would eventually resurface. They simply wouldn't go away. That's why we all need to learn how to deal with our problems head on. Avoidance only makes things worse.

Yes, if you learn how to deal with a challenge head on, you'll save yourself from many sleepless nights and days of constant worry. Besides, my mother's mantra when we were growing up, and to this day is *there is no sense in stressing over things that are out of our control*. In that regard, I learned that half the battle of following my mother's advice was trying to determine what things were actually in my control and what things weren't. But again, I point out that all dots connect. Don't waste time trying to avoid a problem thinking that it will magically go away. It won't.

SERINTY PRAYER

God grant me the serenity to accept the things I cannot change;
courage to change the things I can;
and wisdom to know the difference

****

Here's a list of my ***Top 10 Tools*** that will assist anyone who wants to develop a firm foundation of self. I list them in reverse order so the most important one, No. 1, comes last.

10. <u>Accountability Partners:</u>

Having an accountability partner or Life Coach keeps you on track and consistent with your goal(s). Make sure you don't choose a "Yes" person. By that I mean a person who will say yes and agree to whatever you say or do. Pick an accountability partner who can check and redirect you sternly but with love. Even though I'm blessed enough to have more than one accountability partner, my best friend Andrea has been extremely consistent with me in that role since 1997. Andrea is quick to tell me when I'm right or wrong, regardless of the situation, and regardless of my little feelings.

9. Make Intentional choices/decisions:

Don't do anything "just because". Don't do anything that will benefit only you and may potentially cause harm to other people. Karma will eventually kick in full force when you least expect it. Your intention to make a positive change cannot be solely motivated by trying to prove someone wrong. Of course, it feels good to prove someone wrong when that person has discounted or discredited you. BUT if you are more driven to change because of a person outside of yourself, not only are you choosing to give that person power, you are making a conscious choice to build on an unsure and unstable foundation. If someone is focused in the first place on seeing you fail, nothing you accomplish will ever be enough for them. And guess what? It shouldn't matter. Your life is to be lived and experienced by YOU. Only YOU can decide who plays a part in your life -- and in what capacity.

8. <u>Journal:</u>

Journaling – (writing down your honest and sincere thoughts, feelings, goals) -- is the simplest form of meditation a person can experience. Journaling allows you to take time out for yourself, away from all the noise, and gives you an opportunity to vent. Journaling also helps you think clearly and process your thoughts and daily activities. A lot of us can't complete certain task and goals because we don't take inventory of our thoughts on a regular basis. Journaling is a self-inventory tool that will give you something concrete, something in black and white that will diagram and make clear any progression or regression.

In addition to the journal that I use to jot down random ideas or to plain and simply vent, I also keep a separate gratitude journal. I started a gratitude journal back in 2014. I believe I got the idea from

Elizabeth Gilbert, the author of Eat, Pray, Love during an Oprah Super Soul Sunday interview. Anywhere from once a day to three times a week, I jot down three to five things that I'm grateful for. It reminds me just how many things I take for granted, things that some people would love to have. It's also a good idea to think of things you are grateful for before you go to sleep. It's much better and more productive to go to sleep with pleasant thoughts verses thoughts of stress and tension.

It's easy to forget that everyone does not live with running water, gas, electricity, food, the ability to see, to hear, to speak. Keeping a gratitude journal forces you to seek out something positive every single day. My gratitude journal puts me in a position to stop complaining frequently, and to find some form of joy or freedom on a regular basis.

7. <u>Self-programming</u>:

Reprogramming your subconscious mind will probably be one of the most beneficial things you can do for yourself. We all know people who spend most of their time watching or listening to negative images.

Whether it be watching the news or reality television, playing violent video games, or sharing negative content on social media. People can only feed themselves so much negativity before it starts to seep into their unconscious mind. I've found it to be more beneficial to listen to audio books and motivational interviews. Participate in webinars. In fact, several times a week when I'm driving or working, I listen to spiritual or motivational audio books. I also have an affirmation CD that I listen to from time to time. I enjoy listening to music or occasionally talking on the phone. Better yet, I LOVE music, but improving my subconscious mind holds more weight for me these days. In fact, when a challenge comes your way, anything that will train your brain to reject panic and shift to peace and planning will be beneficial to you. Limit your access to negative verbal and visual images as frequently as possible for your own mental health.

6. Read:

Read daily, even if it's just a small article or passage in a *Daily Word* book (www.dailyword.com). Read something positive and with purpose every day. It'll help shift your perspective on certain issues. A few of my favorite books are, Russell Simmons; *Do You! Super Rich* and *Success Through Stillness*. WM. Paul Young's; The Shack, Don Miguel Ruiz's; *The Four Agreements*, and the *Quest - A Journey of Spiritual Rediscovery* written by Richard and Mary-Alice Jafolla. I always hear my mother suggesting that people read one book of Proverbs a day. Reading daily will also give you an opportunity to learn something new each day.

5. <u>Learn</u>

Learn something new every day. Big or small. A friend of mine texts me a new word of the day, every day, faithfully (Thanks, Kat). Learn a recipe, a new place to travel, an exercise, anything. Be sure to pass on what you've learned on to other people. You'd be surprised at how much of an impact you can have on a person's life by sharing personal lessons that you've learned along the way.

4. <u>Speak/Write Affirmations:</u>

Speak or write down positive affirmations on a regular basis. If time permits, utilize these affirmations daily. If not, make sure that putting positive affirmations into the universe becomes a weekly habit. I AM successful. I AM love. I AM safe and secure. I live in abundance.

3. Take Healthy Risks:

Take some type of a risk every thirty to ninety days. Whether it's taking a class, growing some of your own food or taking a road trip. Just make sure that the risk is promoting your growth. One of my favorite small risks was taking the Mega Bus from Chicago to Minneapolis, Minnesota. I hate taking the bus, but my friend Ashley and I were well on our way when we saw that it only cost $50.00 to $75-00 round trip. In my world, experience wins over risk most of the time. Shake yourself out of your comfort zone consistently. Joining the military, going to college, moving out of state, befriending people who were anywhere from five to thirty-five years older than me -- and traveling outside the United States -- these were all risks that brought me some amazing opportunities.

2. Develop a Budget and Save Money
(See page 78-82 for a few easy-to-use budgeting ideas.)

Sounds weird, but getting a handle of the inflow and outflow of your money will allow you to have more experiences than you'll realize. For several years, when my friends and I traveled, I found that most of my spending money came from spare change that I'd collected over the year. Most of my friends laughed at me and kept the jokes coming because I would pick up every penny I found in the street to throw in my jar. Each time I've cashed out I had $250.00 to $550.00 to use for spending money. I'm currently working on a goal of $1,000 strictly in loose change.

1. <u>HAVE FUN:</u>

Do something fun and enjoyable every day! Yes, I said every single day! One of my favorite things to do every day is watching the old TV comedy "The Golden Girls" ☺ I don't watch much television, but when I do, I'm typically either watching a documentary or a comedy. I only hang out with friends and co-workers who make me laugh. I even have a little class clown trophy from my senior year in high school at Lew Wallace, because I've always believed that laughter truly is the best medication. There are so many fun things available to us. We must make it a point to take advantage of those fun things on a regular basis. DAILY. Life is meant to be lived to the fullest, not observed from afar

CHAPTER 4

Acceptance and Being Present

In this chapter, you will learn how to find the gift in every situation and challenge you encounter. It's my firm belief that this knowledge will prove to be one of your biggest blessings to date. Why is this? It's because once you can accept any tough situation as a lesson, you release the need to resist it. Once you get to the point where you can accept your current circumstances for what they are, you put yourself in a position to move forward and take your next big step in life. Yes! Your next BIG step. Living life fully is about making continuous progression. Progression always moves us forward, but rarely is that movement easy or comfortable.

We do not get to choose how we'll get to our preferred end result. We only get to choose the baby steps we take forward. I will illustrate from my own experiences.

More than once, I had to find the gift within the challenge. For instance, I had to file for bankruptcy with a credit score well over 700. The bankruptcy came about because of a rental property I owned in Indianapolis, IN, with tenants that never paid on time. The most painful time was when I lost one of my closest friend's due to domestic violence (Rest in Heaven, Mia). The day she was taken away from us, I was already in my last few days of work because I had planned to move to Atlanta, Georgia at the time. The plan was for her and her boys to eventually come with.

As much as I hated filing bankruptcy because of that rental property, the bankruptcy put me in the position to clear every debt I had at the time. Being unemployed at the time of my best friend's death, and being determined not to go back to the job I had just left, put me in the position of being able to apply for positions with companies completely out of my comfort zone. I stayed in my next position for over seven years. I don't know if I would have even had the courage to apply if I hadn't first been thrown in the fire, so to speak. I'm not sure if I'll ever understand why Mia's life was taken in such a horrible way, at only 24 years of age, but I accept that her spirit is with me constantly, as well as with both of her boys, her sister Pat, and her niece Tasheena.

One more thing about being dismissed from a position that I had turned into a career. Losing this job was another defining moment in my life. I needed to learn how to take advantage of this supposed difficulty. I had to learn quickly to "become *present*" even without a job. I had to learn that lesson as soon as possible. I had developed a reputation of being hardworking. Not to brag, but I am a person filled with integrity and loyalty-- and I always got the job done. I did so for quite some time. I was specifically requested, on eighty to ninety percent of my cases due to my strong work ethic and my ability to work with difficult families and individuals.

I staffed cases weekly in one of the county offices, attended weekly meetings, was consistently present in court, and participated biweekly in supervision at my own agency. There was plenty of evidence that I worked hard non-stop. I was seen by reliable witnesses working all day every week. Did I mention that my work phone had a tracking device connected? I was both furious and embarrassed by my work being questioned along with other false accusations. But once I realized that resisting wouldn't help my situation, I was free to move on. I stopped giving and making excuses. Then happily, the door was finally open for me to start applying for jobs out of state. Yes, the possibility of moving out of state and making a fresh start was the gift in my storm.

Prior to this incident, I had been talking about relocating for almost 10 years. I had been talking - but not acting. You might imagine correctly that I had made some amazing excuses as to why I couldn't move to another state. The job that let me go via email late at night was one of my favorite excuses for at least seven of those years. Who would take my cases? Would they work with my families as closely as I had? Would I be leaving too many people hanging? Fortunately, I learned quickly that the world keeps moving whether you choose to or not. My cases were reassigned within two weeks.

Once I accepted that my experiences and life there in Indiana were over, I was completely open to start my life's next chapter. Hey, I even applied for positions in Guam and Puerto Rico. About four months later, I moved to Tucson, Arizona, where I live now. I developed a closer relationship with my mother, met some amazing people, took road trips to Mexico, and found a church home, where I was eventually introduced to some amazing and influential people. My Unity church affiliation opened several new doors to me. Writing this book was one of those doors. I became motivated to become certified as a Life Coach and even became involved with a community garden. When it came to gardening, before stepping out of my comfort zone and getting serious about it, all I knew how to do was water plants. Never in a million years would I have guessed that I'd be growing some of my own food in less than two years of my moving away from my comfort zone.

This is just a simple reminder that all steps forward aren't comfortable. Taking big steps is necessary for growth, but those steps won't all be comfortable. Think back in your life. What times do you recall that at first glance seemed terribly difficult, even horrible_____? Recall those times which appeared so bad that you even thought your end was near. How did you get through that time or those times_____? Who did you keep close by your side_____? Was anyone close by your side at all_____? Did you celebrate your victory once the storm had passed_____? Most of you reading this book have experienced some of what I'm talking about. Trust me, we are all much more alike than we are different. You'd be surprised at what some of us have in common.

What are some factors that empower you, that empower us all? I believe they are: learning how to accept what is, letting go of resistance, and embracing the present moment. These factors, and big steps, will empower you to trust yourself with saying yes to new experiences. We get one "go," one big chance at this thing called life. I affirm, that life is meant to be lived, not observed from the sidelines. We must all take chances and get back up after the bumps and bruises that come along with the inevitable hard times.

As we end Chapter 4, I ask you to list below some of your solid fears and solid goals. See if they intertwine. By all means use a separate sheet of paper if necessary. But get down on paper your primary fears and goals. You'll find it helps to have them before you, in black and white to refer to, think about, and act on.

Fears: _____ _____ _____

_____ _____ _____

Goals: _____ _____ _____

_____ _____ _____

"In my life, nothing ever goes wrong. There is a lesson in everything I experience."

~Wayne Dyer (American psychologist, famous author, lecturer and motivational coach)

Balancing the Yin and Yang

Ahhh… the balancing act. For me, life is a balance of holding on and letting go. A balance between the Yin and the Yang, as the Chinese say. Most of us can feel when things are out of whack or off key. One of the best things I've ever heard watching a dialogue between Oprah Winfrey and Iyanla Vanzant was hearing them say, "*At first God throws a pebble and then he throws a brick.*"

I have found that to be true in so many areas. We have to get into the habit of listening to the pebbles and whispers that come our way. The key to maintaining a healthy balance is being able to catch yourself when you begin to feel yourself easing out of the flow. More often than not, we play a big role in a lot of our own long-term suffering. How? By not listening to those whispers and making the choice to remain out of balance longer than necessary.

I've lost count of how many times I've heard people find several years' worth of reasons to remain in unhealthy relationships. Many people (me included) find reasons to go back and forth with eating unhealthy foods, or even continuing to participate in unhealthy habits knowing that those things have the potential to make us really sick. Even though we have times where we do get completely sideswiped, we typically watch things spiral both up and down in baby steps, bit by bit. It's up to us to recognize that spiral and pay attention to which way the spiral is going.

"Having balance is being in harmony with self at all times." Lisa Nichols~ Motivational speaker, best-selling author, business CEO

In order to achieve the harmony mentioned by Lisa Nichols, we need to establish some daily and weekly routines for ourselves. The universe provides us with an abundance of special healthy tools. Just to list a few -- meditation, prayer, keeping a journal, sitting in silence, reading, exercising, drawing, speaking affirmations are among them. We can use any healthy tool that brings us to a state of stillness and causes us to focus on self. Consider a few other tools worth keeping that may work for you. I've played around with a few, but I find that meditation, writing in my journal, and exercising brings be clarity. The next step in developing a sense of balance is paying close attention to your immediate circle.

Back in Chapter 2 I discussed how important your immediate Circle of Influence is. I feel strongly enough about your Circle of Influence that I choose to speak on it again ☺. A true Circle of Influence can help you hold yourself accountable for your actions. My closest friends and some family members are quick to let me know when I'm not myself. This means, among other things: Get rid of YES people during critical times. Keep people around you who are not afraid to let you know when it's time for a push. Keep people around you that care enough to sometimes have just a pinch more faith in you then you do in yourself. Also, keep people around you who remind you when it's time to take a break and have some fun.

Every so often we have to remember the old saying, "Stop and smell the roses." You only get one physical life. Enjoy it. Celebrate every up and learn from every down, learn the gift of letting go. Learning when, who, and what to release at the appropriate time will almost immediately put an end to so much of your long-term suffering. We only get what we allow. Once you get to a place where you know for sure that your peace and sanity are more important than anything else (purchasing this book shows that you're on the right track) you won't accept anything different.

Believe me, it's very possible to love someone from a distance. I've been guilty myself of trying to pour from an empty glass. Not only did that cause me to harbor additional resentments. Pouring from that empty glass put me in a place where I began to hurt people that I loved. I've hurt people and caused problems with past relationships, friendships, and family. In most cases I owned up to my wrongdoing, apologized when I realized an apology was needed, and kept things moving onto the right track.

Indeed, we all are better off when we learn the blessing of balance, and how to develop the steps to total harmony. The daily and weekly routines I listed above are just some of the routines that I use on various occasions in my life.

Here's an important question: What tools do you have in your mental tool box that you keep readily available_____? Do you have any at all_____? If not, I'd like to recommend that you start practicing with three simple practical routines. I believe that all of us are made in God's perfect image. Sometimes life's obstacles knock us off course and cause us to forget that basic, but important fact of life. Developing a set routine will help you remember who you are and what you are capable of. You'll know when you are losing balance.

Different tactics work for different people, so you need to play around with a few options until you discover what speaks to your soul. Again, I believe the three I started with were my gratitude journal, sitting in stillness, and exercise. Then, I noticed that meditation shot up to the top of my list quickly. Whenever you feel out of balance, instead of stewing in your feelings, getting stuck and stagnating, go to your mental tool box. You'll find there the tools to help you find your way back onto the right path.

The first week of 2017, myself and a group of Facebook friends began a weekly gratitude project. This project was something very simple. You can use a mason jar, a small box or a coffee can. On a small piece of paper, we wrote down anything good that happened to or for us that week. Anything that we were grateful for, whether it was waking up, having running water, a new car, home, job, etc. Throw these notes into the jar, and at the end of the fifty-two weeks, read all fifty-two blessings on New Year's Eve. This is just another small tool that will force your subconscious mind to seek out gratitude. And gratitude is far better than indecision and chaos.

CHAPTER 6

Now what? Taking That Next Big Step

So far, we've addressed the importance of having a solid foundation, which includes Acceptance, Balance, Making Peace with Your Past, defining your Circle of Influence, and Leaving Your Comfort Zone (just to list some of the ingredients). Now it's time to physically take steps and make moves. If you've completed any of the exercises and have truly taken these words to heart, you now have a mental and spiritual *Starter Set* of tools to help you withstand tough times, and quickly process any challenges that may come your way.

I'm assuming that by making the choice to pick up this book, either you currently have a challenge that

66|82

you're trying to work through, or you have a set goal with certain obstacles that you believe are holding you back -- or to put it plainly you FEEL stuck. There's one thing that I've learned about God, the Universe, Spirit, Divine, The Most High, Allah, Jehovah, or whatever term you feel most comfortable using. (Some people get really caught up on titles and labels even though most of us are referring to the same great Source.)

What I've learned about the great Source, is that with all these labels, as long as we have a goal or dream that we can visualize, and believe we deserve, there is nothing we can't accomplish. Especially if we have the right tools in place to help us achieve those goals and dreams. We have the power to make our dreams come true. Spirit places everything we need directly in our path. The kicker is that even though everything we need will be laid before us, we STILL need to have courage to take steps to possibly leave behind most of what we have always known.

Yes, we often must leave behind old habits and old acquaintances, among several other things. For example, when I made the decision to go forward with writing this book, I knew within 30 days who I could trust with sharing certain information. Also, once I started telling a few people about my book idea, I was flooded with many helpful resources seemingly out of nowhere (or at least it seemed that way).

Put some thought into whatever your current storm is. Some deep thought. What led up to your current storm_____? Did you see it coming_____? If so, how long did you see that storm on the horizon_____? How does this storm truly make you feel inside_____? Don't avoid what you feel in this moment. We need to acknowledge those feelings in order to take the steps necessary to move past them. There is no such thing as "pushing down or blocking out the pain". Old hurt only festers up later at the wrong time and place, when you least expect it. Working hands-on in the Social Work industry for well over 10 years, I've seen firsthand how a lot of abuse and neglect has come from past unprocessed pain.

Now, put some deep thought into the details of your goals and dreams. The ones you've always felt in the pit of your stomach. Deep inside your gut. The ones placed there by something higher and greater than yourself. What has stopped you thus far from completing those goals and dreams _____? How determined are you to make these things become reality _____? Are you ready to channel your inner courage and make things happen _____? I know that you are ready to make that change because so far, you're still here with me.

Write down one or two specific goals that you would like to accomplish.

1._____

2._____

Visualize the end result of you achieving the goal. Visualize every detail. Your surroundings, the smells, the people around you. You need to be able to actually see proof of these things happening in order to turn them into reality. Now, instead of being overwhelmed with how to accomplish each detail, focus on the daily and weekly baby steps you need to take to achieve your desired end result. For example, if your goal is to lose weight, make an effort to incorporate a fruit or vegetable with each meal and snack. Don't go from lounging on the couch one day to sprinting three miles the next. You'll overwhelm and hurt yourself. You may even feel the urge to give up all together.

The key to accomplishing major goals is to successfully turn those major goals into a series of small tasks. Remain consistent and focused as you complete those small tasks, just as you do when taking one physical step after the other. And be sure to celebrate each victory. You deserve the celebration. But don't get so caught up into the celebration that you lose focus and consistency on the bigger picture.

In the same way, faith by itself, if it is not accompanied by action, is dead.

JAMES 2:17 New International Version. In short *"Faith without works is dead"* 2:14-26

CHAPTER 7

Pay Attention

By continuing to read this book, it shows that you have the discipline and focus necessary to take control of your life. If you don't remember anything else, remember to pay attention to every detail and every sign. Pay attention to your emotions, actions and language. Pay attention consistently. When you feel things are getting out of whack, don't be afraid to stop and regroup. Always remember to center yourself and move forward from a calm space. If you have a strong feeling about anything in particular, remember that there is a reason for it. Also, remember that getting what you need instead of what you want usually trumps all and works out best.

When I made the decision to relocate, I REALLY wanted to move to Atlanta or Texas. Tucson, Arizona was the last place that I wanted to be. The only two people I knew in Tucson, Arizona, were my mother and a young girl from my old military unit. As luck would have it, I got offered a position in Tucson first. A few weeks after I moved, other offers began to roll in. I soon came to realize that Tucson was where I needed to be at that time. Had I moved to Atlanta, Georgia, or Dallas, Texas, I would not have been focused or mentally prepared to pursue my goals in a healthy and responsible manner. None of us are exempt from having bad things happen to us. Challenges are a part of everyone's daily life.

As stated previously, all dots connect. Know that when things are happening to you, they're actually happening for you. Just another thing a picked up from watching one of my many pod cast and interviews. Learn to step outside of your current circumstances in order to see what you need to do next. Nothing happens "just because." I believe that there are no coincidences. Even with most of the bad stuff, some way, somehow, we've played a part in getting into that circumstance. The sooner we can acknowledge our own faults and our own participation in our issues, the sooner we can correct our issues, and transition into our higher selves. You don't need to announce all of your faults to the world, but the least you can do is be honest with yourself.

Acknowledge your weakness and use this new knowledge as building blocks. Everything starts with self. Tune in, and listen to your inner spirit. Prepare to be divinely guided. During my long learning cycle, I constantly received phone calls, text messages, emails, and messages through social media from former clients, colleagues and co-workers. All these messages thanked me for my work and told me how much of an impact I've had in their lives. One previous supervisor sent me a message informing me that a former judge had passed away. My old supervisor remembered how fond of me the judge was; this judge always spoke highly of me and my work. Those many happy messages all reminded me that even though I should have moved on long before, working with positive intentions pay off. When you put love and integrity into your work and life, as I had learned to do, you gain a transformative power.

So, now you're getting ready to fly solo. If you can follow the steps and examples shared with you, along with other useful insights that you will pick up along the way, no other person or situation should be able to steer you off course. You will not give up no matter how tough the circumstances. Hey, I'm not claiming that we are superheroes devoid of doubts and fear. But we are strong spirits utilizing our physical bodies. As long as we have breath, we have the opportunity to face any negative situation and make it positive. The choice is up to you. And I have confidence you're going to make the right choices.

Here are a few parting shots and closing tips. Learn to ask yourself empowering questions. Instead of asking "why me?" ask, "What is this situation supposed to teach me_____?" Ask: "What are some of the gifts I possess_____?" "What qualities do I have that people like most about me_____?" "What do I like about myself_____?" And "What are a few things that I've always wanted to do_____?" Ask "What have I been successful at doing_____?" Ask "What brings me the most joy_____?" THESE are empowering questions. Let go of "Why me".

Remain in a constant state of gratitude. The more you fill yourself with gratitude, the less time you have to focus on stress or anything negative. I sat in a holding cell repeating (mentally) thank you. I was grateful that even though the correctional officers were taking their sweet time, I knew that I would eventually be bonded out with my ride waiting in the lobby (at 4:00 a.m.). Ninety-five percent of the people sitting in the cell with me weren't so lucky. Gratitude and meditation got me through.

In the end, I've enjoyed a few winters without snow. Not only were the utilities and past due mortgage issues taken care of at my home in Gary, Indiana. But the mortgage was paid several months in advance. I beat the worse part of my court case, I'm currently a Certified Professional Life Coach, and now I AM an author! As usual, all Is well -- and I affirm that everything works out to my best benefit. Whether you are aware of it or not, most times, things will work out to YOUR best benefit as well.

James Baldwin, the great writer and philosopher, said it: *"Not everything that is faced can be changed, but nothing can be changed until it is faced."*

With Much Love,
Lalita ☺

Final Thoughts written by: Naz Khalid

I never talk about what I "wish" I could do anymore. Because I know now that dreams and wishes are simply goals unrealized and or things that we don't believe we deserve.

I think about what it is I want.

I hold the thought positively.

I write it.

I say it out loud.

I imprint my intention on the universe.

I get busy doing what I need to do to make it happen and allow the universe to conspire with me.

I know that the only thing standing between me and the life that I want, is ME.

So, I refrain from making excuses, stand in my personal power, and make a way for the life that I want. I am doing it unapologetically, vigorously, passionately, and gently without stepping on others but rather lifting others up as I work towards getting there. This is a wonderfully beautiful journey. Ase'

#ICanDoAnything #SideBlindersOn

Sincerely......
Naz Khalid www.nazkhalid.com

Just a few people I'd like to thank!

Whether I sell 10 copies or 10 million copies of this book, there are a few people that I must thank, due to their part in inspiring me on this personal journey of mine.

Blonde.: (My mother.) Thank you for showing me what strength -- physically, emotionally and spiritually -- looks like. You showed us that it was possible to hold it together even when a person's entire world could change overnight. Because of that, I don't think that there is any obstacle that can defeat me.

Ree-Ree and Nora. (My sister and cousin.) Thank you! Even when I didn't realize it, you've always had my back and supported me. You've showed constant love and acceptance with every choice that I've made. Neither of you ever judged me or made me feel less than. I really appreciate that, and I know that I can ALWAYS count on you two.

Andrea-Chief. (My best friend.) Thank you! You continue to show what it means to be a best friend. You've done that since we were 14 or 15 years old.

I've always been a little odd/different. You've accepted each of my odd ways and never made me feel like there was anything I needed to change (outside of me having a smart and sometimes harsh mouth ☺). You are always the first person to keep every secret and the first person to let me know when I'm wrong without sugar-coating it. I love you for that. You've always been more of a family member than a friend. Thank you. Proverbs17:17 says: *A friend loves at all times.*

Barbara and Molly. You two alone hold the torch for making me realize that I had the potential to make any of this possible. You showed me in a very short time that I could become a Certified Life Coach, an author, grow my own food and do anything else that I really wanted to do. Thank you

Unity of Tucson: Thank you for teaching my how to embrace my power within. I learned the true meaning of the scripture in James 2:17: *...faith by itself, if it is not accompanied by action, is dead.* (N.I.V.)

References and Suggestions

Additional Materials:

Bi-Weekly Coin Savings Chart: (Based on 26 pay periods)
Feel free to double it!

ROLL OF QUARTERS	$10	$260
ROLL OF DIMES	$5	$130
ROLLS OF NICKELS	$2	$52
ROLLS OF PENNIES	.50	$13
		TOTAL: $455.00

Figure #1

12 Month Vacation Funds: (Wedding, Debt Payoff, New Car, Moving, Home Repairs, Etc.)

Month	Saved Amount
January	$50
February	$100
March	$150
April	$75
May	$125
June	$100
July	$125
August	$100
September	$100
October	$150
November	$75
December	$50
Total	$1200

Figure #2

Dave Ramsey's 7 Baby Steps:

www.daveramsey.com

Baby Step 1- $1000 to start and Emergency Fund

Baby Step 2- Pay off all debt using the Debt Snowball

Baby Step 3- 3 to 6 months of expenses in savings

Baby Step 4- Invest 15% of household income into Roth IRA's and pre-tax retirement

Baby Step 5- College funding for children

Baby Step 6- Pay off home early

Baby Step 7- Build wealth and give!

Track/Budget Every Dollar: (Create a separate list, chart, due date calendar)

1. Mortgage/ Rent-
2. Utilities
3. Savings
4. Life Insurance
5. Health Insurance
6. Child Support
7. Credit Cards
8. Tithes
9. Groceries
10. Car repairs
11. Student Loans
12. Misc.

January
(Document Due Dates & Keep them posted)

Sun	Mon	Tue	Wed	Thu	Fri	Sat
						1
2	3	4	5	6	7	8
9	10	11	12	13	14	15
16	17	18	19	20	21	22
23	24	25	26	27	28	29
30	31					

Figure #3

Figure #4

Things I'm Grateful for Today
1.
2.
3.
4.
5.
6.
7.
8.
9.
10.
11.
12.
13.
14.
15.

Figure #5

DESIRE/GOAL	FIRST (BABY) STEP	AFFIRMATION
Example: I desire to lose 20lbs	I will include a fruit or veggie with every meal.	I've lost weight in a healthy manner before and I will do it again. I AM 20lbs lighter

Made in the USA
Las Vegas, NV
13 March 2021

19503186R00049